DRAWING IS EASY!

DRAWING DINOSAURS

Written & designed by Anton Poitier

Illustrated by Hui Yuan Chang

Published in 2022 by Windmill Books,
an Imprint of Rosen Publishing
29 East 21st Street, New York, NY 10010

Illustrated by: Hui Yuan Chang

Cataloging-in-Publication Data

Names: Poitier, Anton, author. | Chang, Hui Yuan, illustrator.
Title: Drawing dinosaurs / written by Anton Poitier, illustrated by Hui Yuan Chang.
Description: New York : Windmill Books, 2022. | Series: Drawing is easy!
Identifiers: ISBN 9781499487268 (pbk.) | ISBN 9781499487282 (library bound) | ISBN 9781499487275 (6 pack) | ISBN 9781499487299 (ebook)
Subjects: LCSH: Dinosaurs in art--Juvenile literature. | Drawing--Technique--Juvenile literature.
Classification: LCC NC780.5 P65 2022 | DDC 743.6--dc23

Printed in the United States of America

CPSIA Compliance Information: Batch BSWM22: For Further Information contact Rosen Publishing, New York, New York at 1-800-237-9932

WINDMILL BOOKS

Let's get started!

This book shows you how to draw dinosaurs by drawing shapes. There are steps to draw every dinosaur. There are also lots of hints and tips for making your drawings different!

Get drawing!

1 Begin by drawing the first shape in the center of a piece of paper.

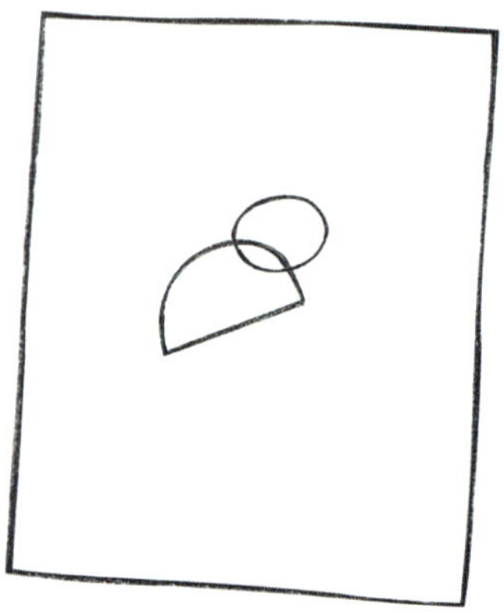

2 Draw the second shape where shown.

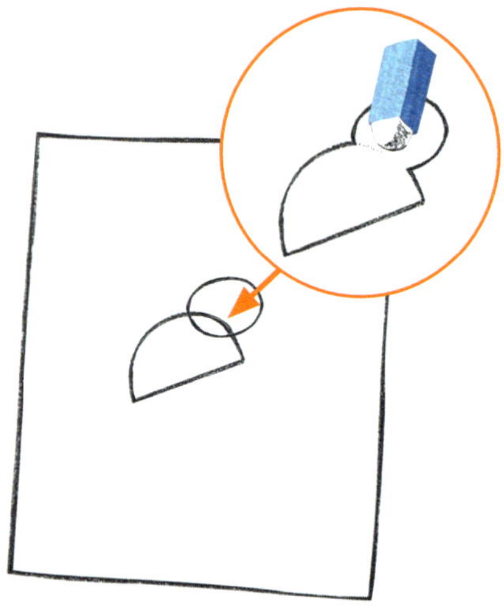

3 Erase the pencil marks where they overlap.

Tips to make your dino special...

Using colored pencils

Here are some handy tips. You can use colored pencils, felt-tip pens, crayons, or watercolor paints to complete your drawing. Water-soluble colored pencils work very well. The pictures in this book are colored in this way.

Mix and match!

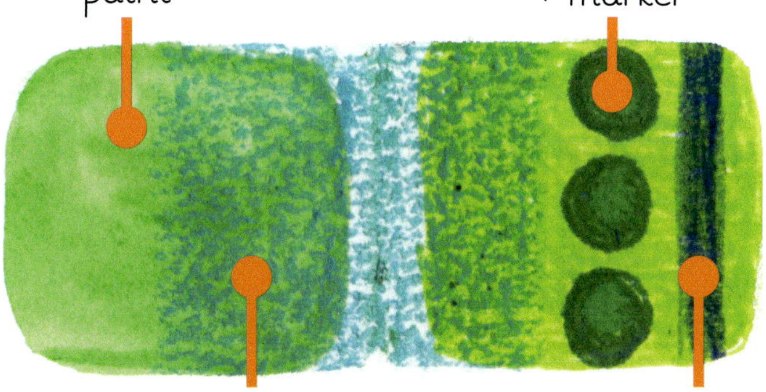

Draw a scary T. rex

T. rex had short arms with two claws on each. He used them as hooks to catch his prey. Yikes!

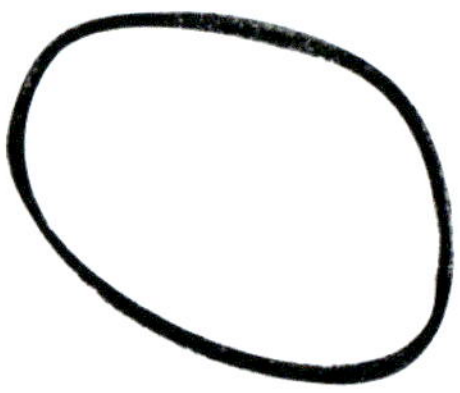

Draw his head like this.

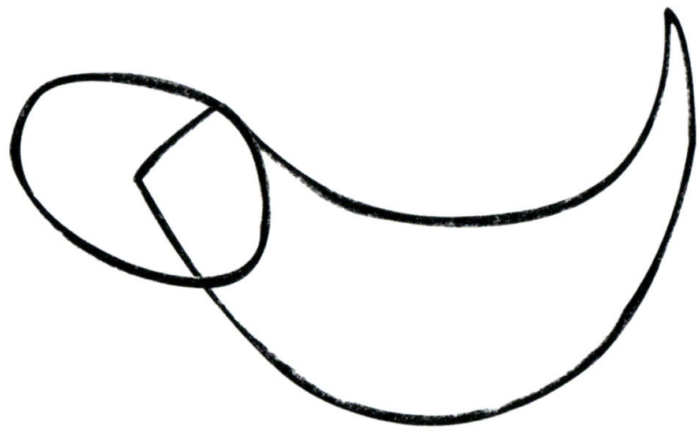

1. Draw the head.
2. Add the body.

3. Now draw the front legs.
4. Add the back legs.

Draw a zigzag along my back.

Color me with paints or colored pencils.

Add a ROAR too!

Make me any color!

Draw an open mouth!

Make your T. rex look different!

Give me sharp teeth!

Notice the position of the body and head.

Flip the shapes so that the T. rex faces the other way.

I'm in a museum!

Sketch a Stegosaurus

The Stegosaurus could be 30 feet (9 m) long, but had a walnut-sized brain!

1. Draw the Stegosaurus's head.

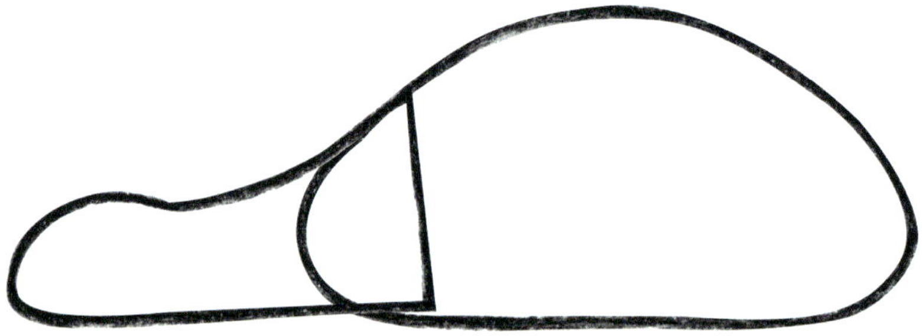

2. Add the body to the right of the head.

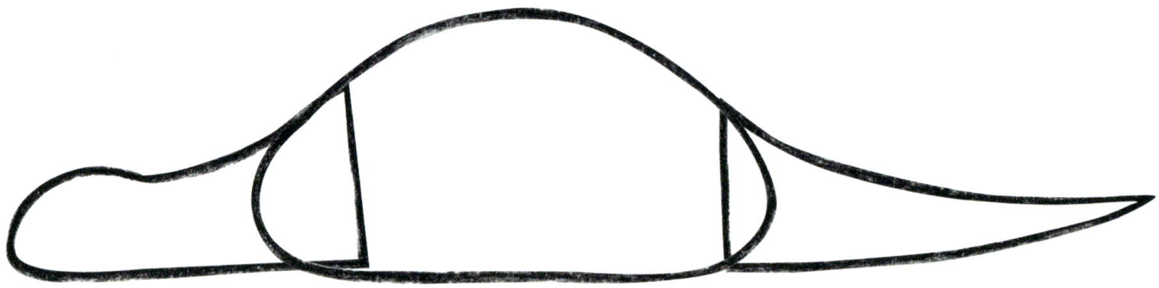

3. Now draw the tail.

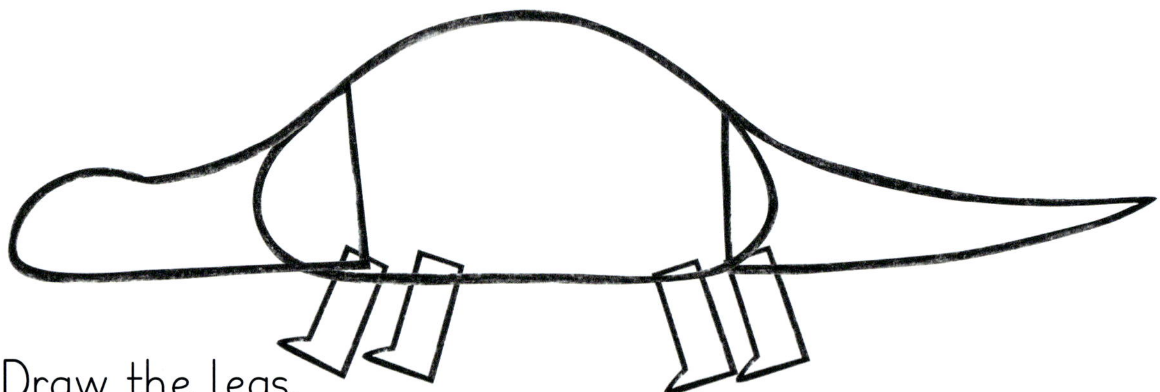

4. Draw the legs.

Draw spines along my back.

Invent a pattern for the body.

Color your dinosaur with paints or colored pencils.

Use your favorite colors!

You could give me diamond-shaped spines!

Give your dinosaur a smile!

Straight legs

Make your Stegosaurus look different!

Draw an open mouth.

Flip the body the other way.

Draw a Brontosaurus

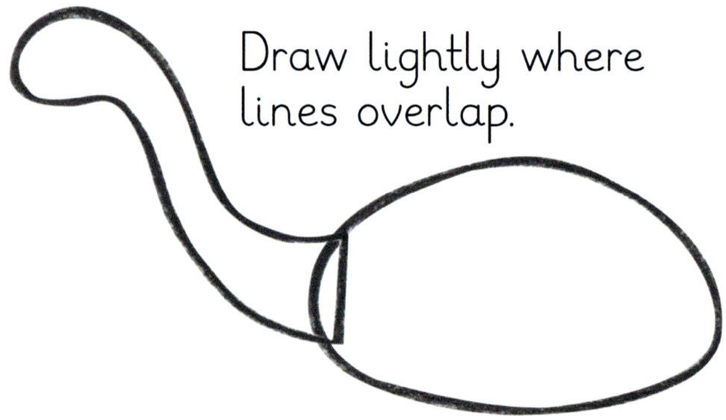

Draw lightly where lines overlap.

1 Draw the head and neck.

2 Now draw the body.

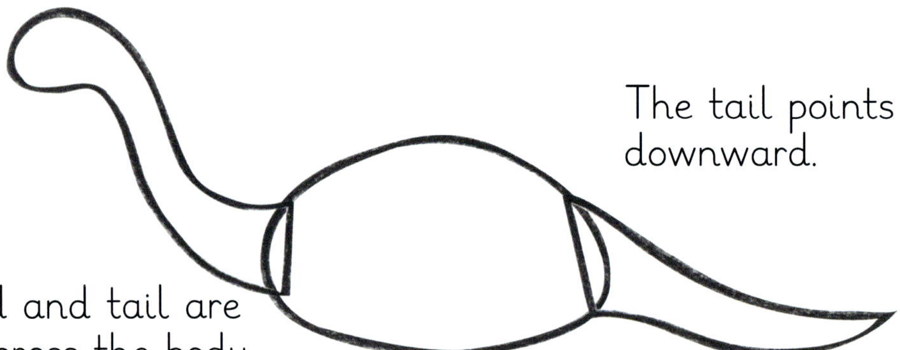

The tail points downward.

The head and tail are in line across the body.

3 Add the tail next.

The legs go straight down.

4 Draw all four legs.

Some people call me by a different name: Apatosaurus. I was over 75 feet (23 m) long!

Give your dinosaur a happy face!

Color your dinosaur with paints or colored pencils.

Make your Brontosaurus look different!

Flip the shapes to make the dinosaur face the other way.

I like the sea!

Draw a spiky Triceratops

Draw lightly where lines overlap.

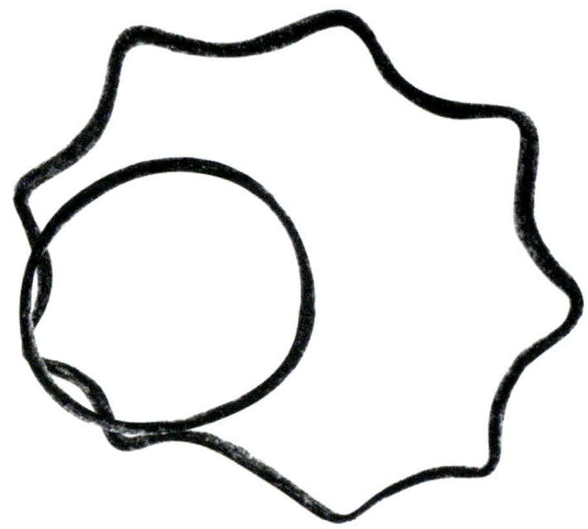

1 Draw the dinosaur head.

2 Add the frill that goes around the head.

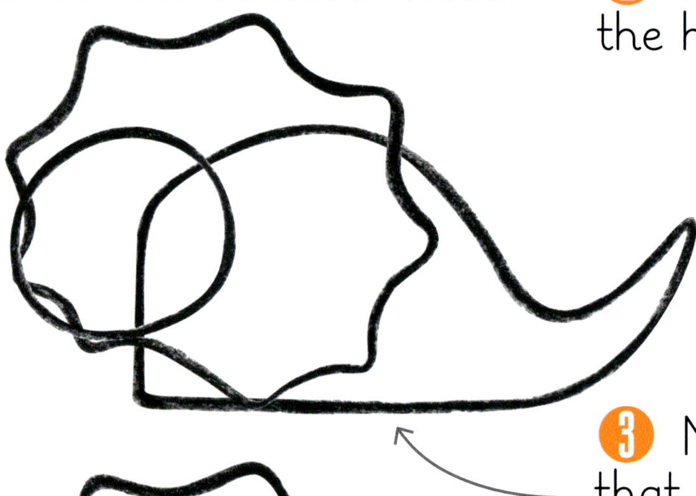

3 Now draw the body so that the bottom edge lines up with the bottom of the frill.

4 Add four legs.

Draw an open mouth.

My name means "three-horned face" and I was about 30 feet (9 m) long!

Add eyes, nostrils, and horns!

Your Triceratops can be any color you like!

Make your Triceratops look different!

Alter the leg positions.

Head the other way around

It could be facing you, like this one.

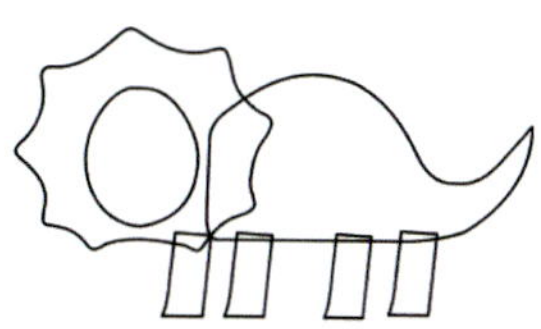

Draw an Ankylosaurus

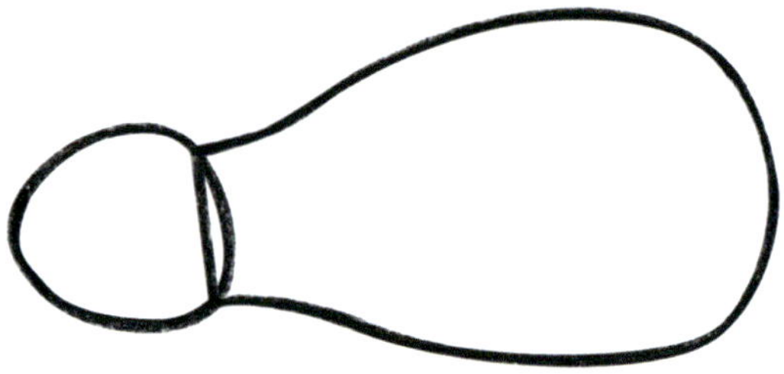

Draw lightly where lines overlap.

1. Draw the dinosaur's head.

2. Add the front part of its body.

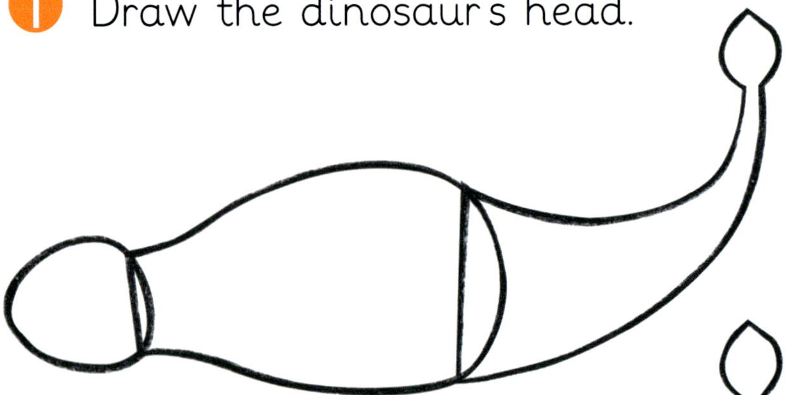

3. Then add the second part of the body.

4. Draw the front legs.

5. Add the back legs.

Make your dinosaur look friendly by copying this mouth shape.

Give me lots of spikes all over my body!

Add some flowers to eat.

I used the club at the end of my tail to bash other dinosaurs!

Make your Ankylosaurus look different!

Draw a fierce face!

Tail facing downward

I was about 30 feet (9 m) long!

Tip the body forward.

Change the leg positions.

Draw a Diplodocus

Draw lightly where lines overlap.

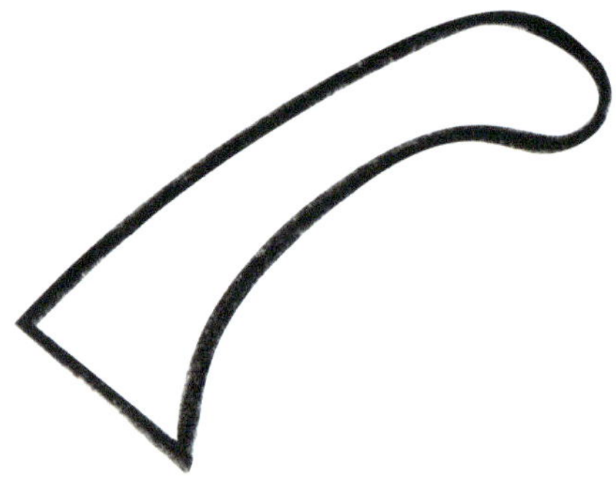

1 Draw the Diplodocus's head.

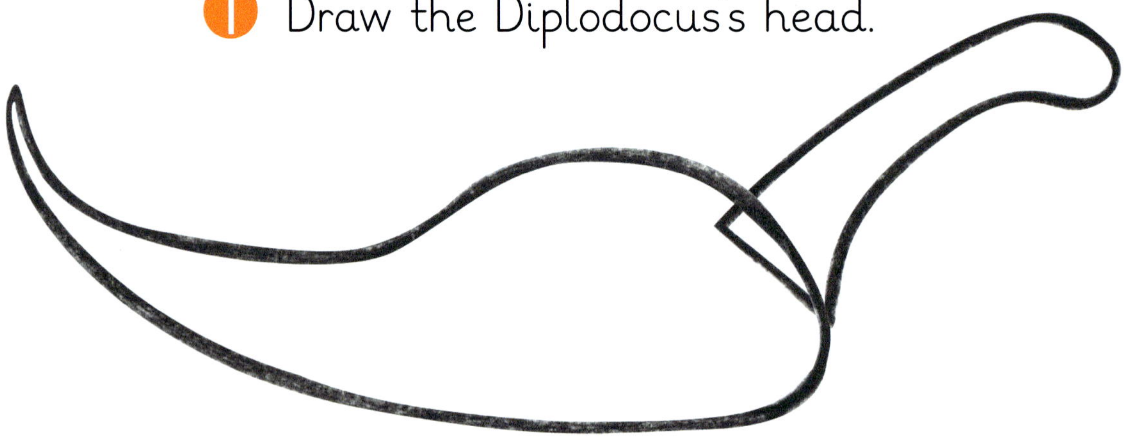

2 Add the body.

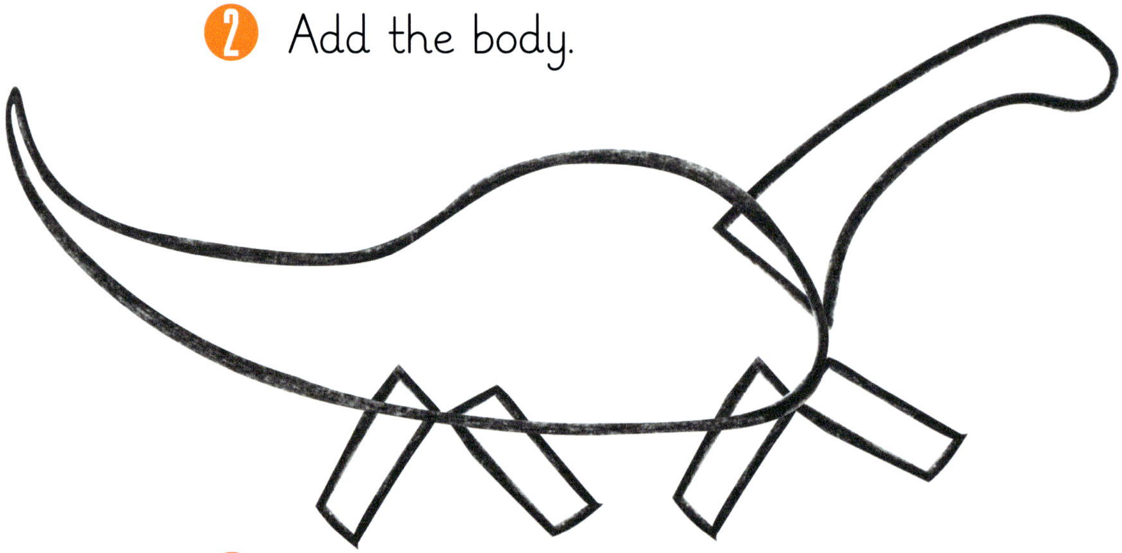

3 Now draw the legs.

Diplodocus was about 115 feet (35 m) long – the length of 7 cars parked end to end!

Give your dinosaur a pattern on its back.

Add some flowers.

Make your Diplodocus look different!

Turn the body upside down to make your dinosaur look like this.

Draw little trees to make your dinosaur look huge!

Change the leg positions.

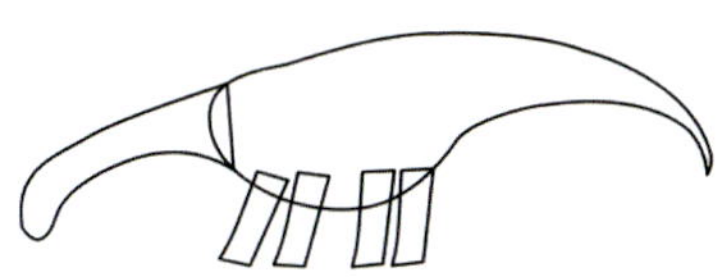

Draw a Velociraptor

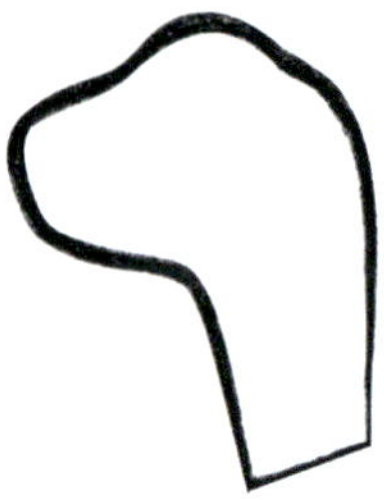

Draw lightly where lines overlap.

I'm called a Vel-ah-sih-rap-tor.

1 Draw the dinosaur's head.

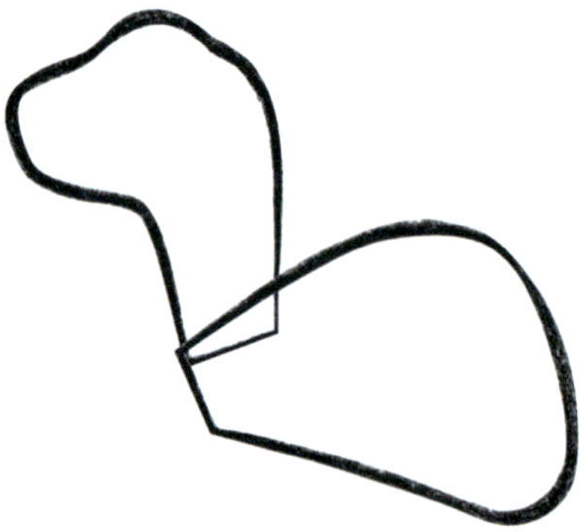

2 Next, add the body.

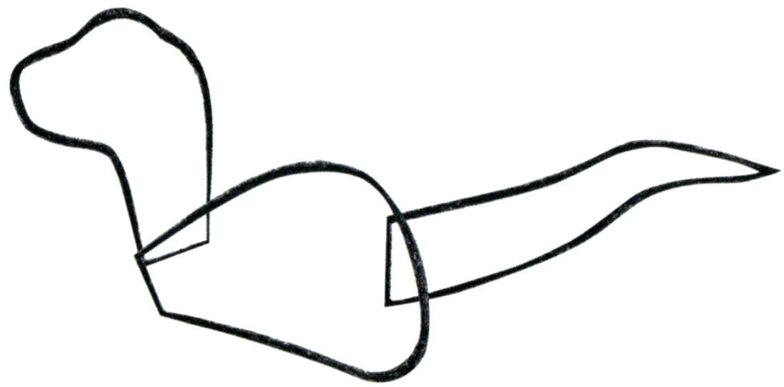

3 Then draw the tail.

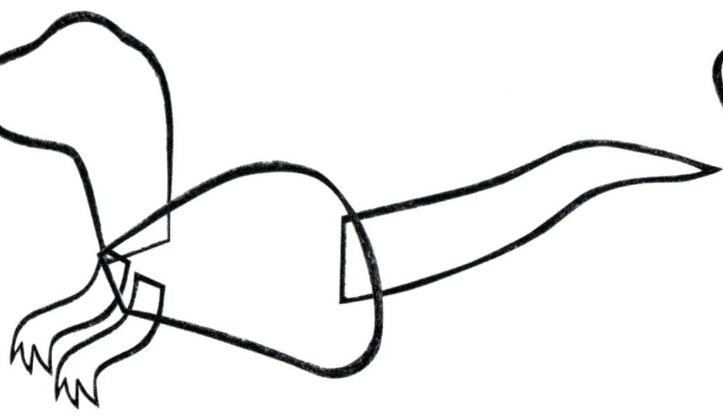

4 Add the front legs.

5 Draw the back legs.

The Velociraptor was about the height of a Labrador retriever and had sharp claws to kill its prey.

Add sharp teeth to make a fierce dinosaur!

Turn the head around.

Make your Velociraptor look different!

Draw open jaws.

You could give your dinosaur spots or stripes. No one knows the true color of any dinosaur!

Draw a Corythosaurus

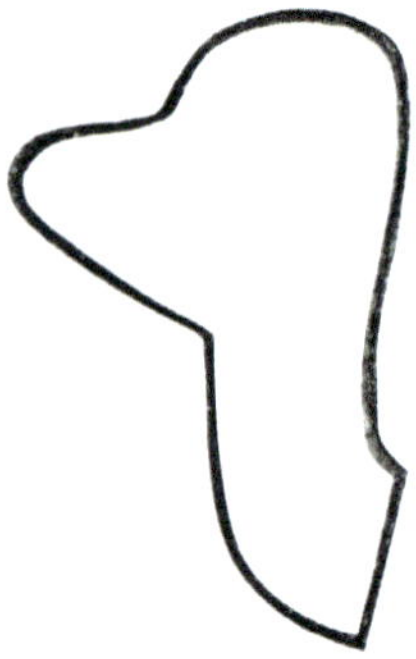

Draw lightly where lines overlap.

1 Draw the dinosaur's head.

I'm called a Ko-rih-thoh-sore-uss.

2 Next, add the body.

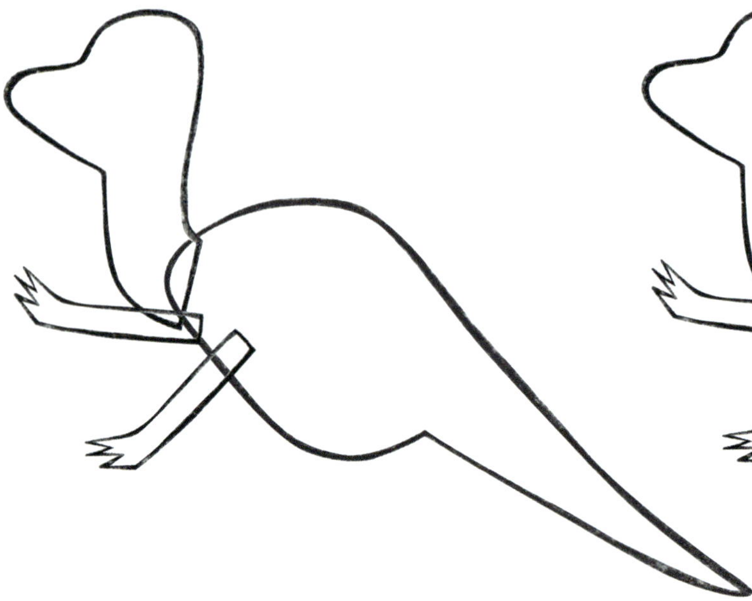

3 Add the front legs.

4 Now draw the back legs.

My name means "helmet head," after the helmet-like crest on top of my head. People think this was used to make a loud horn noise.

I like to eat plants!

Choose your favorite colors!

Stripes look good!

Make your Corythosaurus look different!

Draw stripes on the helmet and back.

Change the leg positions.

Draw the body angled upward.

Draw an Icthyosaurus

Draw lightly where lines overlap.

1 Draw the creature's head and middle part of its body.

2 Next, add the tail.

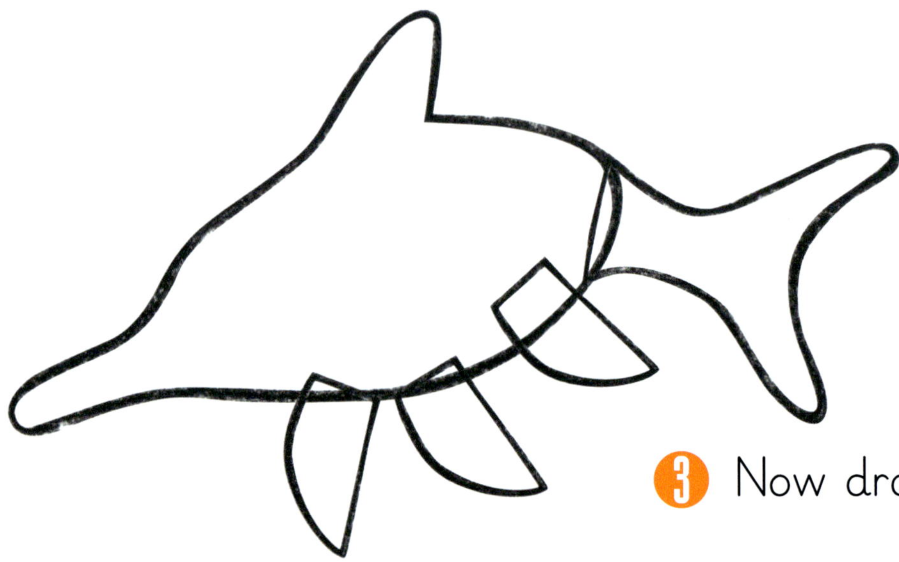

3 Now draw the fins.

My name means "fish lizard" and I gave birth to live babies, not eggs.

Color your Icthyosaurus so that the mouth is open.

Make your Icthyosaurus look different!

Make an open mouth by changing the head shape a bit.

Change the tail position.

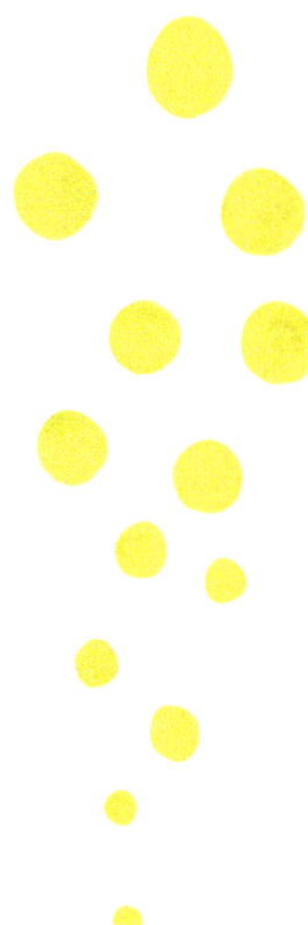

Draw spots or stripes.

Add bubbles.

Draw a Plesiosaurus

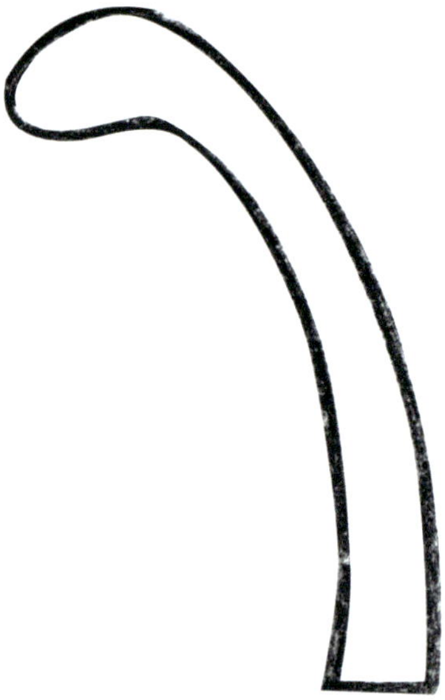

1 Draw the creature's head.

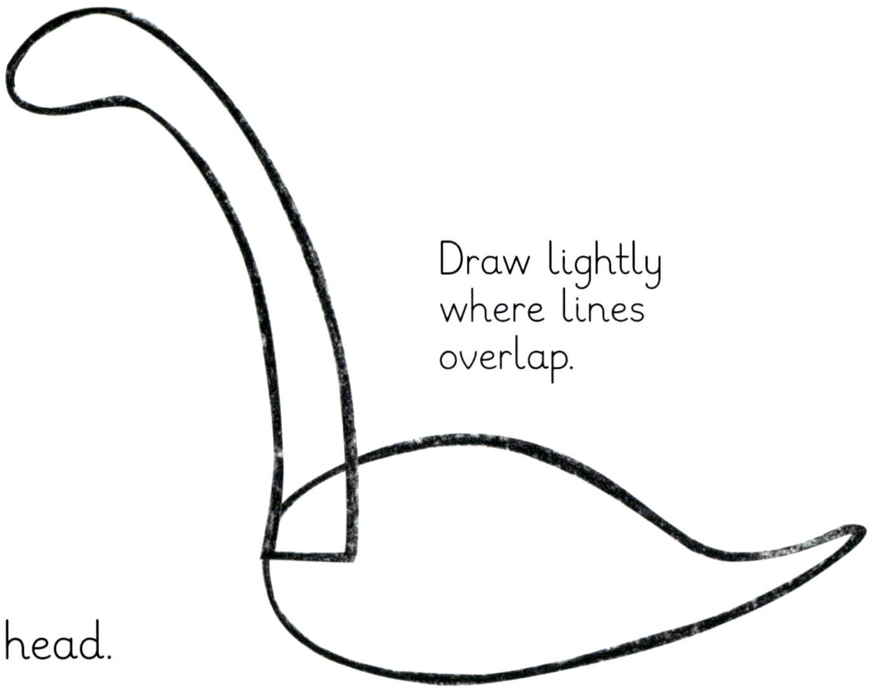

Draw lightly where lines overlap.

2 Next, add the body.

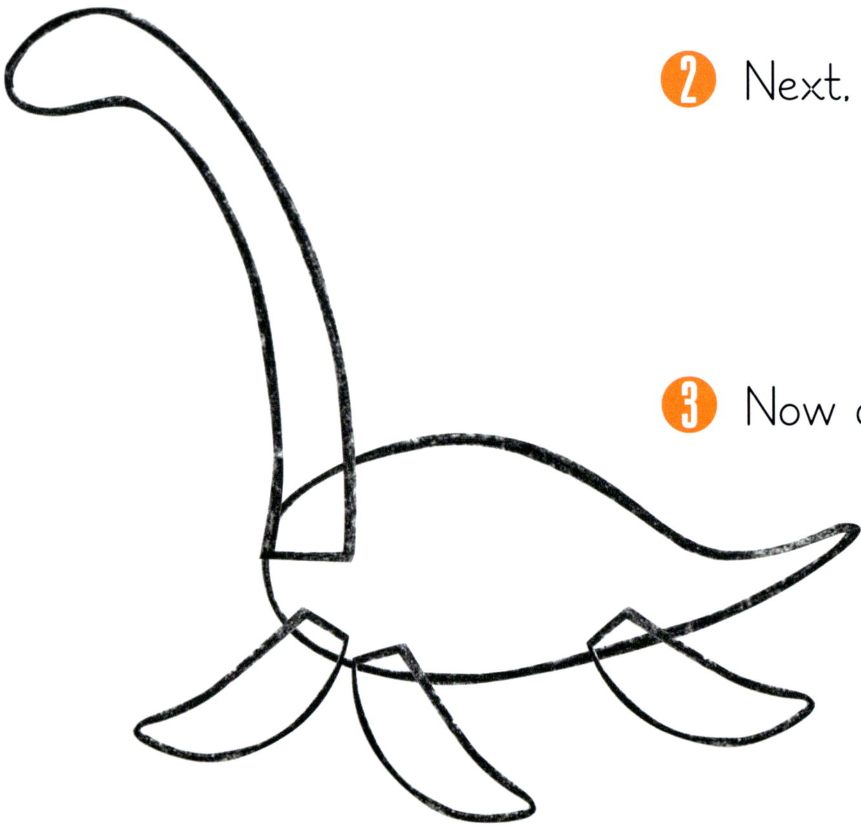

3 Now draw the fins.

Plesiosaurus lived in the sea. It had sharp teeth and grew to about 55 feet (17 m) long.

People who believe in the Loch Ness Monster think it is like a Plesiosaurus.

Plesiosaurus lived until about 65 million years ago.

Make me happy or fierce!

Make your Plesiosaurus look different!

Add a flying saucer!

Add water for your creature to swim in.

Draw a Pterodactyl

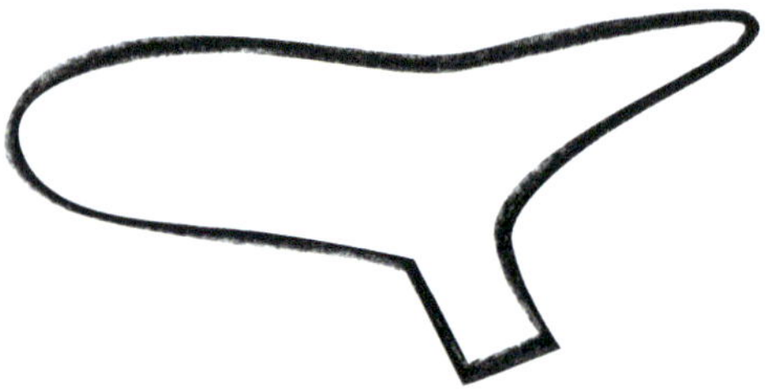

1 Draw the creature's head.

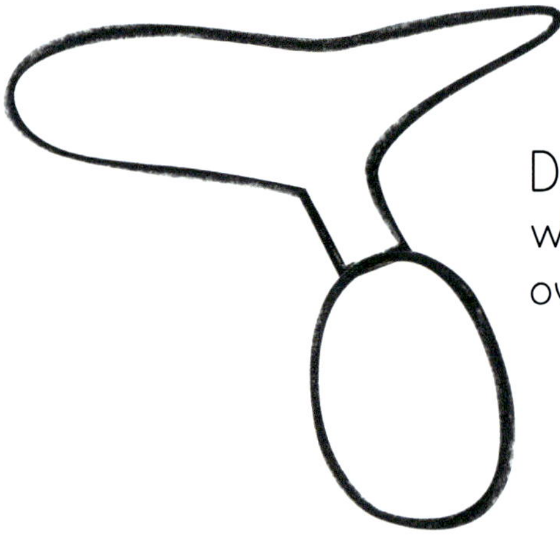

Draw lightly where lines overlap.

2 Next, add the body.

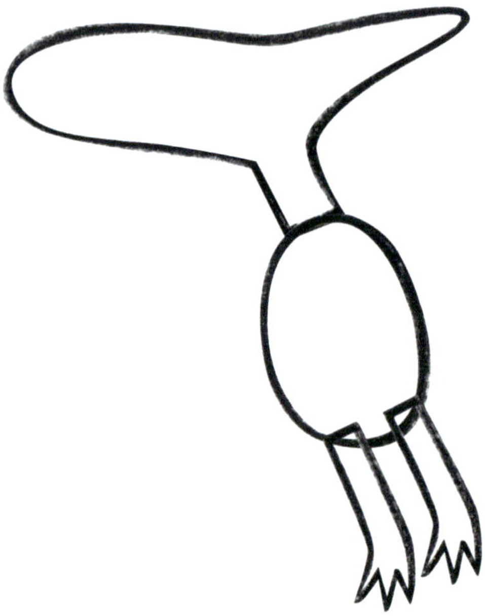

3 Add the two legs.

4 Add the wings and tail.

My name mean "winged lizard."

Add sharp teeth.

Color the wings so that you can see the bones.

Draw a fish in the jaws.

Make your Pterodactyl look different!

Turn the wings around so they flap downward.

Change the angle of the head.

Draw the legs straight out instead of downward.

Choose your favorite colors!

Pterodactyls had a wingspan of up to 36 feet (11 m)!

Draw a Spinosaurus

1 Draw the dinosaur's head.

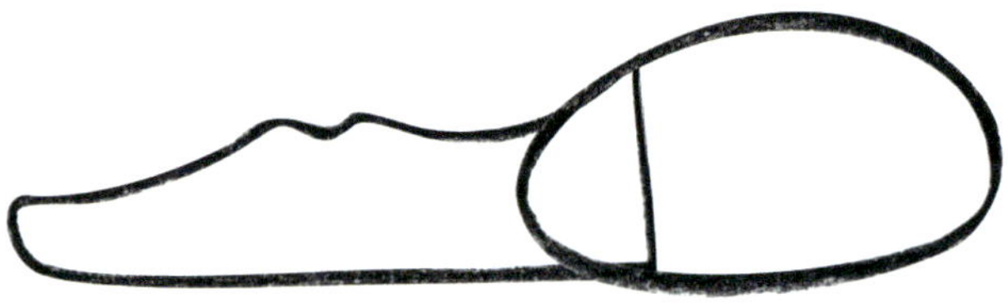

2 Next, add the body.

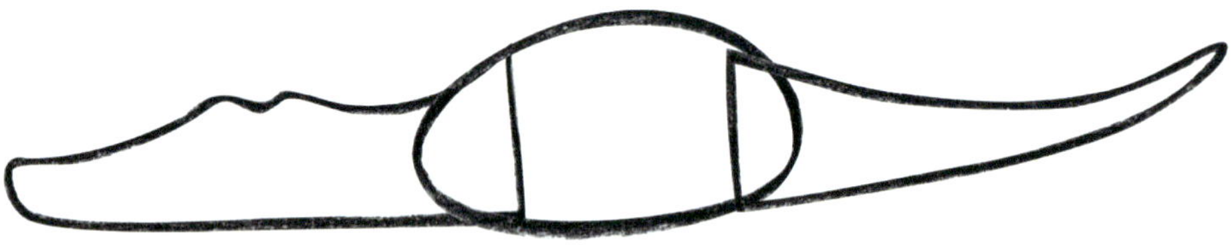

3 Add the tail.

Draw lightly where lines overlap.

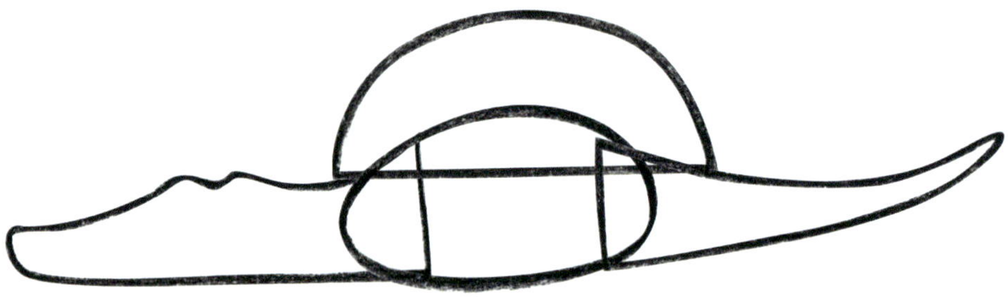

4 Now draw the spine shape.

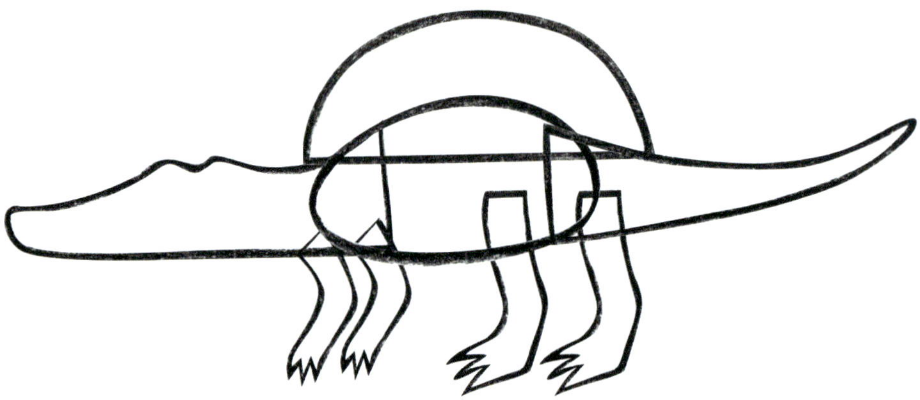

5 Then draw the front and back legs.

Spinosaurus was larger than T. rex and may have been the biggest meat-eating dinosaur ever!

My name means "spine lizard."

Add some water too!

Make your Spinosaurus look different!

Draw some trees and a volcano to add scenery to your picture.

Add sharp teeth!

Change the angle of the tail and head to make the drawing like this.

Draw an Iguanodon

1 Draw the dinosaur's head.

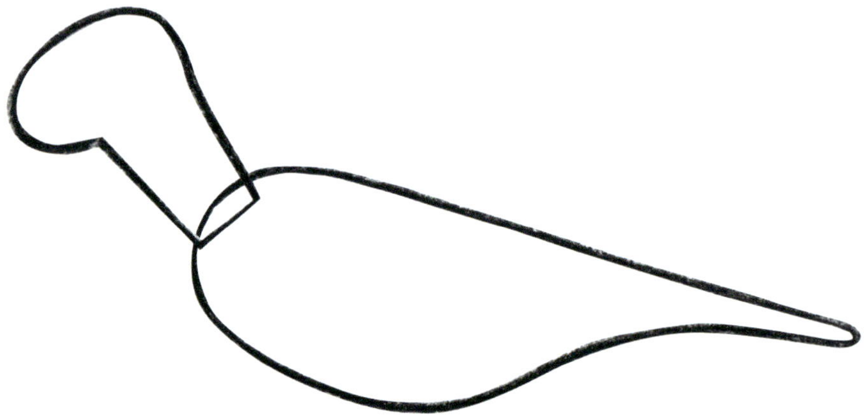

2 Next, add the body.

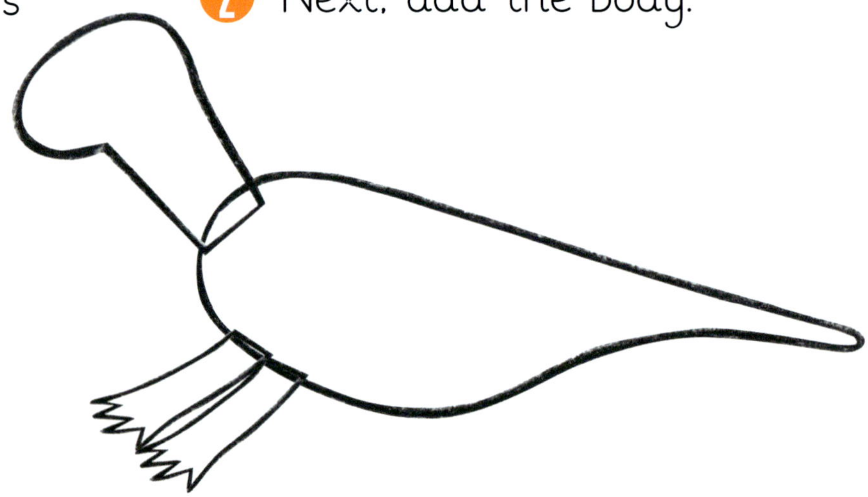

3 Add the two front legs.

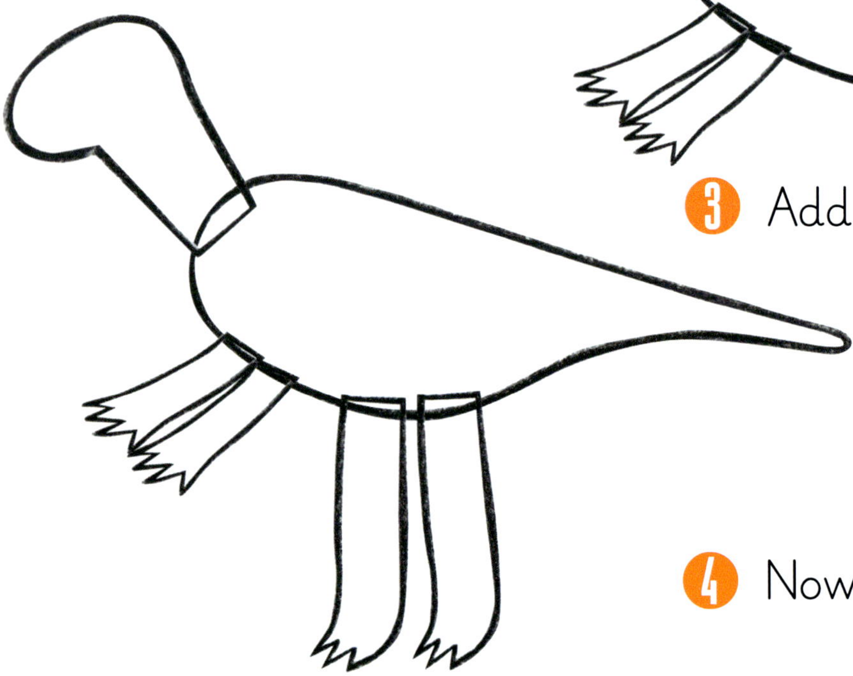

4 Now draw the back legs.

You could color your Iguanadon to make it into a funny character! Add instruments to make a band!

Iguanadon ate plants, grew to 40 feet (12 m), and weighed as much as a van!

Draw spikes along the dinosaur's back.

Draw a jacket, bow tie, and hat!

Make your Iguanadon look different!

Turn the head around.

Change the leg and arm positions.

Add clothes and a hat!

Draw a Dimetrodon

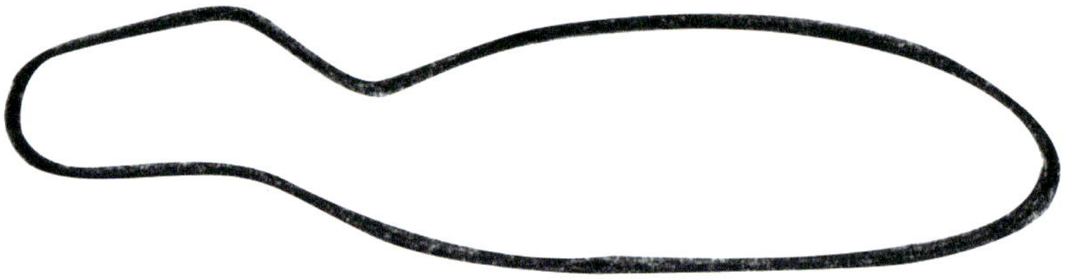

1 Draw the head and body.

2 Next, add the tail.

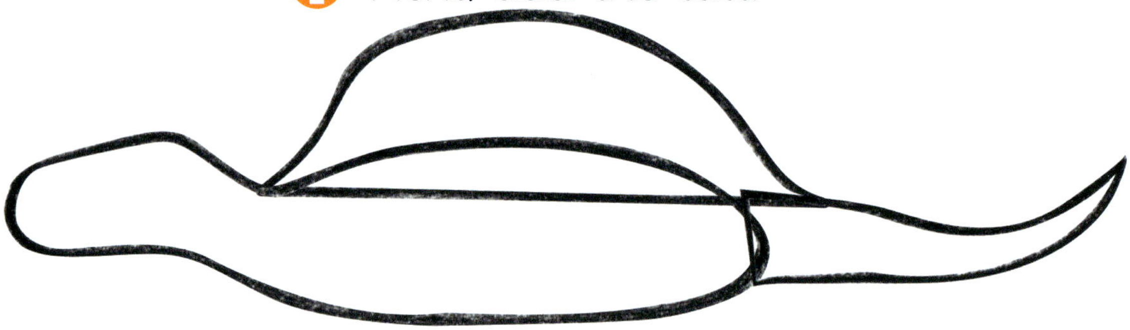

3 Add the sail shape.

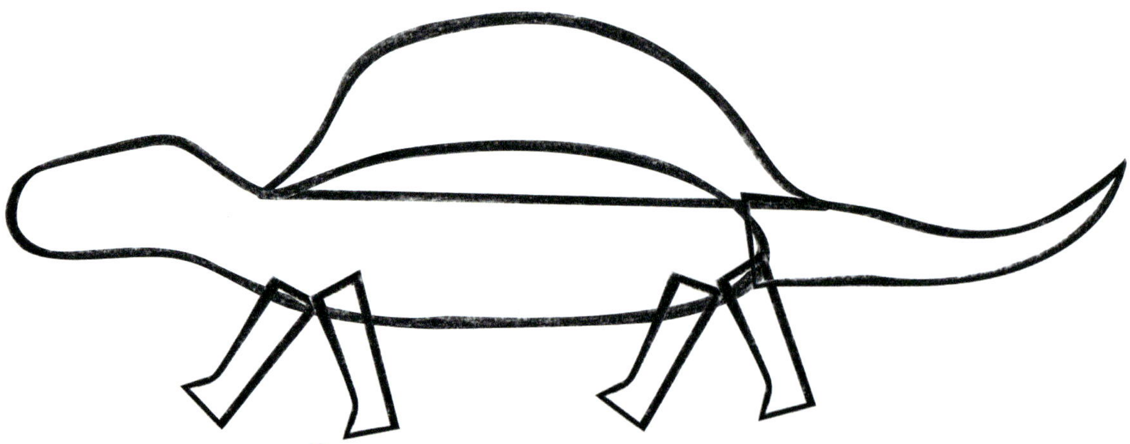

4 Now draw the legs.

Complete your creature with your favorite colors.

Color spikes in the sail shape on the back.

Dimetrodon ate meat and grew to about 15 feet (4.5m).

Add teeth to make it fierce!

Make your Dimetrodon look different!

This one looks happy!

Make the sail any shape or color you like!

Dimetrodon is a bit weird - people think of it as a dinosaur, but it existed before the dinosaurs came along!

Draw a Doyouthinkhesaurus

You can invent your own crazy dinosaur by using shapes from different creatures in this book. Give your dinosaur a funny name. Here's how to draw a Doyouthinkhesaurus!

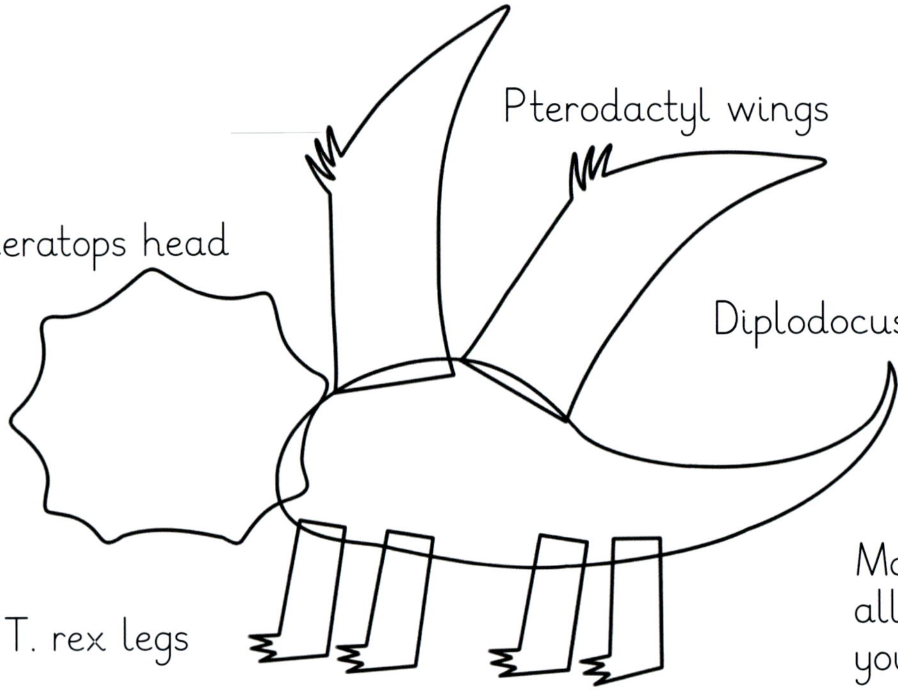

Make a display of all the dinosaurs you've drawn using this book.

Choose colors and patterns for your creature!

You could draw lots of different crazy dinosaurs by mixing up the shapes in this book!